# Fly High with Novel Units

Dear Teacher,

Novel Units use children's literature to expose students to the pleasure and enjoyment of books within the reading period. Novel Units are often taught in place of the basal lessons for a period of time. Our booklets focus on help for the teacher. They are not workbooks, although a few pages may be copied for student use. Novel Units are collections of comprehension questions, bulletin board ideas, and integrated subject activities, which use the latest in reading strategies and graphic organizers.

We have enjoyed preparing the units which will provide new ways to teach reading, thinking, writing and the love for literature. Add your own ideas to reach your special class and make reading in your room a celebration.

The Authors

## Novel Units

P.O. Box 1461
Palatine, IL 60078

Telephone (708) 253-8200
FAX: (708) 253-8240

ISBN 1-56137-123-8

Hatchet

by

Gary Paulsen

STUDY GUIDE

by

Gloria Levine, M.A.

**Note:**
A Puffin Book edition of <u>Hatchet</u> published by the Penguin Group was used to prepare the Teacher Guide. The page references may differ in other editions or in the hard back book.

# Hatchet

## By Gary Paulsen

**Summary**

Thoughts of his parents' divorce fill Brian Robeson's head as he flies in a single-engine plane to visit his father in the Canadian wilderness. When the pilot suffers a massive heart attack and dies, Brian must land the plane. He crashes over a lake and Brian struggles to get to the surface of the water. Left with only the clothes he is wearing and a hatchet he received from his mother, Brian must find a way to survive.

**Instructions Prior to Reading: Setting The Purpose**

Previewing the book: Have students examine the cover. Ask: How old does the boy appear to be? What sort of expression does he have on his face? After reading the question printed on the lower right hand corner of the cover, what can you guess about the airplane shown in the picture? What are some things the boy might use the hatchet for? What is the animal shown? What do you think happens when that animal appears in the story? Do you know what the silver circle showing the three figures means? (The book is a Newbery Honor book.)

Given the following clues from the cover, write a paragraph predicting what you think will happen in the story.

—a hatchet  —a boy  —a plane  —wilderness  —lost and alone

**Prereading Discussion Topics**

Learning new skills: Have you ever been faced with an unusual problem which required you to learn some new skill or skills? What was the situation? How did you feel at first? What skills did you lack? How did you learn these skills? How did you feel when the whole thing was over?

Facing a frightening situation: Have you ever been in a situation where Nature frightened you (such as finding that electricity was cut off by a storm, or that a hurricane raged around you, or that you were lost in the woods, etc.) What made you afraid? What did you think about? How did you overcome your fear?

Thinking positively: Have you ever heard the expression, "the power of positive thinking"? What does it mean? Do you believe in it? If not, why not? If so, when have you seen it work for someone else? When has it worked for you?

Patience: Think of a time when you needed to have a lot of patience. Describe the situation. Was it difficult to have patience? Why or why not? What was the outcome? Is patience always a good thing to have?

Relationship of people to nature: What rights do you think animals and plants in the wild have? Do you think humans have the right to kill wild animals? If so, when? What is your opinion of hunting and fishing?

**Prereading Activities**

1.  Make an attribute web with students for the idea of "survival." Students may want to add to the web as information in the story unfolds.

    Begin by writing the word "SURVIVAL" in the center of a large piece of paper. Ask students to quickly tell what "Survival" makes them think of. On "wheelspoke-lines" from the central word—survival—list student ideas. Encourage students to elaborate on particular ideas, and show them how to depict these subcategories on the web. (See the sample web below.)

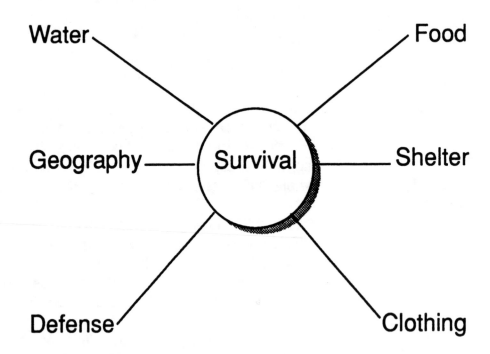

2. Tell students to imagine that they find themselves alone in the wooded wilderness. Divide students into five panels, each responsible for coming up with ideas for one of the following: food, shelter, clothing, recreation, signaling for help. A spokesman for each panel summarizes the panel members' ideas for the entire class.

3. Have students fill out the following questionnaire by marking each statement "A" for agree or "D" for disagree. After the story is read, students should discuss whether they would give the same responses.

1. _____ If your parents do something to make you angry, you should talk to them about it.

2. _____ Secrets should not be told.

3. _____ A wild animal will not bother you unless you bother it.

4. _____ Sometimes life is so hard it would be better not to go on living.

5. _____ Feeling sorry for yourself doesn't help anything.

6. _____ The best way to learn is from your mistakes.

7. _____ It is better to wait and have patience than to rush into things.

8. _____ To keep on top of things, stay positive.

**Bulletin board
or Activity Sheet**   A major theme of the story is how Brian learns to cope with fear.
Have students graph the degree of Brian's fear after each chapter
in the story.

| chapters | not at all afraid | learning to be brave | trying to be brave | afraid | terrified |
|---|---|---|---|---|---|
| 1 | | | | | |
| 2 | | | | | |
| 3 | | | | | |
| 4 | | | | | |
| 5 | | | | | |
| 6 | | | | | |
| 7 | | | | | |
| 8 | | | | | |
| 9 | | | | | |
| 10 | | | | | |
| 11 | | | | | |
| 12 | | | | | |
| 13 | | | | | |
| 14 | | | | | |
| 15 | | | | | |
| 16 | | | | | |
| 17 | | | | | |
| 18 | | | | | |
| 19 | | | | | |

**Prediction and
Recommended
Procedure Sheet**

<u>Using Predictions in the Novel Unit Approach:</u> We all make predictions as we read--little guesses about what will happen next, how the conflict will be resolved, which details given by the author will be important to the plot, details will help to fill in our sense of a character. Students should be encouraged to predict, to make sensible guesses. As students work on predictions, these discussion questions can be used to guide them: What are some of the ways to predict? What is the process of a sophisticated reader's thinking and predicting? What clues does an author give us to help us in making our predictions? Why are some predictions more likely than others?

A predicting chart is for students to record their predictions. As each subsequent chapter is discussed, you can review and correct previous predictions. This procedure serves to focus on predictions and to review the stories.

**Predicting what
will happen**

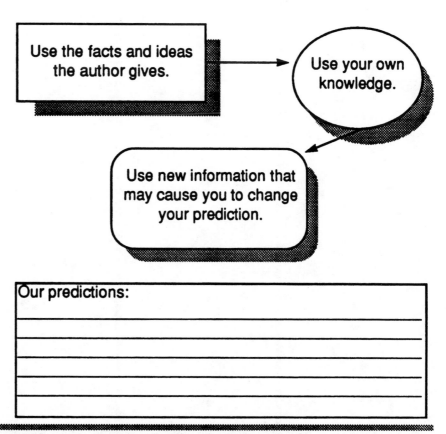

FLY HIGH WITH NOVEL UNITS ©1989 Dr. Anne Troy, Ph. D. and Phyllis Green, M.A.

**Prediction Chart**

| What Characters have we met so far? | What is the conflict in the story? | What are your predictions? | Why did you make those predictions? |
| --- | --- | --- | --- |
| | | | |

**Chapters 1 and 2**
**pages 1-25**

**Vocabulary**

| | | |
|---|---|---|
| banked 5 | tundra 7 | lashed 7 |
| wincing 7 | turbulence 13 | cowling 15 |
| altitude 22 | transmissions 23 | impact 24 |
| visualize 24 | | |

**Exercise**    Extend the following synonym chains

1. turbulence—tumult—violence—_____ _____ _____

2. wincing—cringing—flinching—_____ _____ _____

**Discussion**
**Questions**
**and Activities**

1. Where is the plane taking Brian? Why? *pp. 6 and 7 Brian is on his way to see his father in Canada, a month after his parents' divorce?*

2. How does the pilot treat Brian? *p.1-The pilot is quiet, p.4- but friendly, allowing him to take over the controls.*

3. What was Brian's mother's gift to him when he left? *p.8 a hatchet* How did he feel as he accepted the gift? Why? *p.9 He was angry at his mother, but felt guilty for not speaking to her, so he tried to sound grateful and to hide how ridiculous he felt putting the hatchet on his belt.*

4. What happens to terrify Brian? *p.12 The pilot has a heart attack.*

5. How does he handle the emergency? *p.15-He uses what he has learned to try to keep the plane's nose up, p.16-tries to send a radio message for help and p.23-looks for a clearing to land in.* What would you do? Would you be as calm as Brian is?

6. How is Brian like you? How is he different. Make a T-comparison chart.

| Brian | You |
|---|---|
| | |

**Prediction**    Do you think Brian will be able to land the plane or will it crash?

**Story Map Flow Chart**

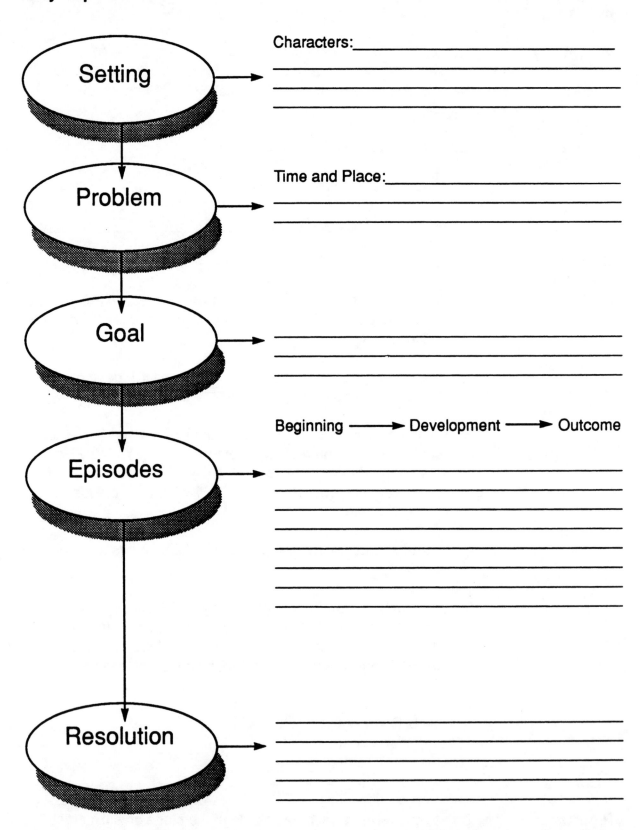

Characters:_____
_____
_____
_____

Time and Place:_____
_____
_____

_____
_____
_____

Beginning ———→ Development ———→ Outcome
_____
_____
_____
_____
_____
_____
_____
_____

_____
_____
_____
_____

**Using Character
Attribute Webs**     Attribute webs are simply a visual representation of a character
from the novel. They provide a systematic way for the students to
organize and recap the information they have about a particular
character. Attribute webs may be used after reading the novel to
recapitulate information about a particular character or completed
gradually as information unfolds, done individually, or finished as a
group project.

One type of character attribute web uses these divisions:

How a character acts and feels. (How does the character feel in
this picture? How would you feel if this happened to you? How
do you think the character feels?)

How a character looks. (Close your eyes and picture the
character. Describe him to me.)

Where a character lives. (Where and when does the character
live?)

How others feel about the character. (How does another
specific character feel about our character?)

In group discussion about the student attribute webs and specific
characters, the teacher can ask for backup proof from the novel.
You can also include inferential thinking.

Attribute webs need not be confined to characters. They may also
be used to organize information about a concept or object or place.

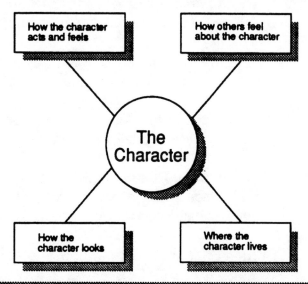

**Chapters 3-4
pages 26-42**

**Vocabulary**

| | | |
|---|---|---|
| wallow 27 | wrenching 28 | abated 33 |
| massively 35 | grazed 35 | remnants 36 |
| hordes 36 | naturalist 38 | hammocks 39 |

Have students develop a word map for "abated," using the
following form:

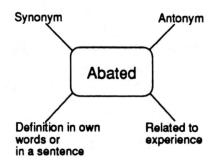

**Discussion
Questions
and Activities**

1. Why is Brian looking for a lake? *p.27-He knows that to land in
   the trees would mean death.*

2. Who is it that Brian hears screaming as the plane crashes?
   *p.29 himself*

3. Why doesn't Brian drown in the crash? *p.29 He escapes
   through a window, rises to the surface, and swims to the bank.*

4. What is "The Secret" and how does it make Brian feel? *p.32
   Brian feels anger and hatred whenever he remembers seeing
   his mother with a man who was not Brian's father.*

5. As the sun comes up, Brian's eyes become swollen shut within
   moments.  What is the cause?  *p.37 mosquitoes*

6. How does Brian feel as he looks around at the scenery? *p.41
   He is still in a daze, but finds it pretty.*

**Drama Activity**   In a monologue, there is only one speaker, who reveals his thoughts
and feelings. Pretend that you are Brian. In a monologue, describe
what has happened to you and how you feel about it.

**Prediction**   When Brian wakes up, what will he do?

FLY HIGH WITH NOVEL UNITS ©1989 Dr. Anne Troy, Ph. D. and Phyllis Green, M.A.

**Chapters 5-6**
**pages 43-66**

**Vocabulary**

| | | |
|---|---|---|
| foul 43 | extensive 47 | amphibious 48 |
| motivated 50 | lean-to 57 | diminish 57 |
| ruefully 65 | | |

Complete the following analogies using words from the vocabulary list above. One is done for you.

Cold is to Hot as Black is to White
Alertly is to Sleepily as Happily is to _____ (ans:Ruefully)
Vegetable is to Carrot as Shelter is to _____(ans:Lean-to)
Soften is to Harden as Grow is to ____ (ans: Diminish)
Thin is to Fat as Narrow is to ____ (ans: Extensive)

**Discussion Questions and Activities**

1. Brian is thirsty and does something he knows he shouldn't. What is that? What is the result? *p.45 He intends to drink only a little, but gulps the lake water, and throws up as a result*)

2. Brian feels overwhelmed by the rush of confused thoughts that he has. What does he tell himself to calm himself down? *p.46 Take one thing at a time; keep your thoughts short.* Can you think of a situation you might find yourself in where this advice would be useful?

3. What happened before the plane crashed that might make it more difficult for searchers to find Brian? *p.53 The pilot had jerked the pedal, making the plane fly off course.*

4. Why does Brian think of Mr. Perpich? Do you think Mr. Perpich's advice is good? *p.49 Brian is trying to stay positive, the way his English teacher always suggested.*

5. List everything Brian has when the plane crashes. Rate the items, with 1=the item that you think is most valuable to him NOW, 2=next most valuable, etc.)
(change, a fingernail clipper, a billfold with a $20 bill, paper, a hatchet, the clothes he is wearing, a watch).

6.  Describe the shelter Brian decides to build. What other kinds of shelters could he make? What kind would you make? *p.56 He decides to make a lean-to in a sheltered area, covered with leaves and sticks.* Begin Problem Activity

| Problem | Solution Attempts | Outcomes |
|---|---|---|
|  | 1. |  |
|  | 2. |  |
|  | 3. |  |
|  | 4. |  |

7.  Brian wonders what there is to eat. What idea does the TV show Brian once saw give him? What mistake does Brian make when he first finds food? *p.61 The woman in the show found beans on a bush, so Brian looks for berries.*

**Art Activity**      Make a collage (using magazine cut-outs, drawings, even real objects) that shows all the items Brian has with him when the plane crashes.

**Prediction**      How will Brian solve the problem of how to start a fire?

**Chapters 7-8
pages 67-86**

**Vocabulary**       welted 69          receded 70          rivulets 77
                     seepage 77         gingerly 81

Use words from the vocabulary list to fill in the blanks in the
sentences below.

1. After the rain, _____ (rivulets) ran down to the lake.
2. His face was _____(welted) with mosquito bites.
3. He _____(gingerly) felt the spot where the quills had entered
   his leg.
4. His hunger first sharpened, then _____ (receded).
5. He let the _____ (seepage) from the bag of berries drip into
   his mouth.

**Discussion
Questions
and Activities**

1. What mistake does Brian make that is like the mistake he made
   when he drank too much water? *p.67 He eats too many sour
   berries and gets sick.*

2. Why is Brian so upset about what he saw in the mall? What do
   you learn about the Secret that you did not know before? *p.68
   Brian's mother was kissing the stranger.*

3. Why is Brian frightened by his reflection in the water? *p.69 His
   face is bleeding, his hair is matted.*

4. Why isn't Brian worried about eating the new kind of berries?
   *p.73 He recognizes them as raspberries from when he and
   Terry used to eat them in the park.*

5. What problem does Brian run into while he is berry-picking?
   Why doesn't he run far away? Would you? *p.75 Brian sees a
   bear. He decides that the bear does not want to hurt him.*

6. How does Brian become injured? How could he have avoided
   getting hurt? *p.80 A porcupine shoots quills at Brian when
   Brian throws his hatchet at it.*

7.  After the attack, Brian learns the most important rule of survival. What is that? *p.82 Feeling sorry for yourself doesn't work.*

8.  How does Brian get his idea for starting a fire? Do you think the idea will work? What steps would you take to start a fire if you were in his place? *p.86 When Brian sees the spark from the hatchet as it hits the stone, he realizes he could use such a spark to start a fire.*

**Writing Activity**          Think of a time when you felt sorry for yourself. Write a composition about your situation and why it did or didn't help to feel sorry for yourself.

**Writing/Art Activity**          Make a "missing person's" poster for Brian. Include such important information as his physical description and where he was last seen. For a "photo" use a magazine cut-out, or draw your impression of what Brian looks like.

**Prediction**          How will Brian's life change once he has a fire?

**Chapters 9-10
pages 87-102**

**Vocabulary**

| | | |
|---|---|---|
| haunches 87 | registered 88 | tendrils 88 |
| flammable 88 | depression 90 | smoldered 90 |
| flue 93 | eddied 95 | dormant 99 |

Circle the word that does NOT belong with the others and explain why.

1.  haunches, tendrils, legs, knees (ans: tendrils are little curls; all the rest refer to the legs)

2.  flammable, incendiary, flaming, dormant (ans: dormant means inactive; all the rest refer to fire)

3.  smoldered, eddied, circled, swirled (ans: smoldered refers to burning; all the rest refer to a circling motion)

**Discussion**
**Questions**
**and Activities**

1. Brian figures out how to make sparks, but he still has other problems to solve before he will have a good fire. What are the problems? *p.87 finding tinder to ignite, p.92 finding something to keep the fire going*

2. How does he finally start the fire from the hatchet sparks? (p. 89-He uses thin bark slivers for tinder, *p.92- dried grass and wood pieces to feed the flames, and dead tree limbs to keep the fire going.*

3. Who is Brian's hungry friend? *p.92 the fire*

4. Why can't Brian leave the fire? How does he solve the problem? *p.94 He needs to keep feeding it so that it will not die out. p.95 He makes a large woodpile near his shelter.*

5. What are the clues that the sounds Brian heard at night were made by a turtle? *p.97-There are tracks coming up from the lake to the sand and p.98-whatever made the tracks had a dragging bottom, feet that stuck out, and laid eggs in the sand.*

6. Does Brian like the taste of the eggs? Why does Brian stand so that he cannot see the eggs, after eating a few of them? *pp.101-102 He doesn't like the taste at first, but grows used to it, and wants to keep himself from eating them all at once.*

**Writing Activity**     Write a composition about a time that you had to keep trying for a long time, making many mistakes, before you were successful at something.

**Prediction**     Will Brian keep hoping to be found?

**Chapters 11-12**
**pages 103-118**

**Vocabulary**

| | | |
|---|---|---|
| flailing 110 | tapered 111 | hefted 111 |
| telegraphed 111 | motive 112 | |

Answer each of the following questions with a "yes" or "no."

1. When you sign your name, are your arms flailing? (no)
2. Is an ice cream cone tapered? (yes)
3. Does a feather need to be hefted? (no).
4. Is water a motive for thirst? (no).
5. Can you telegraph the answer "no" with a shake of your head? (yes)

**Discussion**
**Questions**
**and Activities**

1. Why does Brian bother to clean his camp? Would you? *p.104 He finds that when he is busy he has less time to feel depressed.*

2. How is Brian's body changing from the way it was before the crash? *p.104 He is thin, now, and tan.*

3. How long does Brian work on the fish spear? What is the result? *p.111 He works for hours on it, but it does not work.*

3. How is Brian's mind different now? Are the changes good? *p.105 He sees more, hears more, and his mind and body are more connected.*

4. When does Brian begin thinking about his mother's baked chicken? Why? *p.114 When he sees the bird fly out of the leaves, he thinks about how good it might taste.*

5. What happens to make Brian lose hope that he will ever be found? *p.117 A plane passes overhead, but no one sees his fire or hears his cries.*

**Writing Activity**

Imagine that Brian had kept a list in the sand of "things to do." What would his list say?

Imagine that you keep a list of "things to do." What would your list for this week say?

**Game Idea**    Suppose you are the boy and you decide to make up some ciphers to pass the time. In certain ciphers, numbers are used to take the place of letters. For example, if a=1, b=2, c=3, etc. then "Hello" becomes 8-5-12-12-15. Write a sentence in cipher telling one thing you have learned since your plane crash. Give the sentence to a partner and see if he or she can decipher it.

**Prediction**    What new dangers will Brian face?

**Chapters 13-14
pages 119-136**

**Vocabulary**    rectify 128        corrosive 130        impaired 130
                  wedging 132

Match three of the words in the vocabulary list with their opposites, in the antonym box below.

> soothing  improved  worsen

(ans: soothing-corrosive; improved-impaired; worsen-rectify)

**Discussion
Questions
and Activities**

1. How are Brian's feelings when he sees the wolf like his feelings when he saw the bear? *p.121 In both cases, he is frightened at first, then realizes the animal does not want to hurt him.*

2. How many days have passed since the crash? *p.122 47*

3. When did he try to kill himself? Why? *p.122-5 days after the crash he had lost hope and wanted an end to the misery.*

4. Who is the "new Brian" and what two things does he know that the old Brian did not? *p.123 Brian thinks of himself from the morning after the suicide attempt on as the "new Brian"; he realized that morning that he would never be the same and that he would not die.*

5. What are two mistakes Brian makes? Why do you suppose he mentally lists them to tell his father? What does this show you about him and about his father? *pp.123-124 He nearly blinded himself with his new bow and at first he couldn't catch any fish.*

6. How does something Brian learned in science class come in handy when trying to catch fish? Have you ever learned something at school that you found surprisingly useful in "real life"? *p.125 Brian realizes that the reason he keeps missing the fish is because of the refraction of the light, so he starts aiming the arrow at where the fish is, not where it appears to be.*

7. What is tough hope? Have you ever had tough hope? *p.127 belief that you can help yourself, even if others cannot help you.*

8. Describe a mistake that at first is funny, but in the end nearly kills Brian. How does Brian show that he learns something from the mistake? *p.130 Because the lean-to is not sturdy enough and the eggs are within reach, a skunk finds his way in and sprays Brian, blinding him for several hours. p.131 He improves his shelter by weaving logs together, and puts his food on a shelf out of reach of animals.*

9. How does Brian solve the problem of finding enough fish to eat? *p.135 He makes a pen in the water for storing fresh fresh.*

**Literary Analysis:**
**Theme**                    One clue to theme (an important statement the author is trying to make through his story) is often what a character learns. What has Brian learned about small mistakes? *p.128 In a survival situation, it is important to keep alert, because even small mistakes can turn into disasters.*

**Prediction**               What new skills will Brian acquire?

**Chapters 15-16
pages 137-160**

**Vocabulary**     camouflage 139     stabilize 142     rotate 145
grimace 154

Below are four definitions. Fill in the blank next to each with the vocabulary word that it defines. Then write four sentences, each including one word from the list.

_____ (stabilize) keep steady

_____ (rotate) turn

_____ (camouflage) disguise

_____ (grimace) make a contorted face

**Discussion
Questions
and Activities**

1. What does a "First day" mean to Brian? Name three of his "First days." What are three of the most important "First days" you have had in your life? *p. 137 A first day is an important day he uses as reference to remember time--the day of First Meat (foolbird), the day of First Rabbit, and First Arrow day.*

2. Why is the day Brian washes the dead bird in the lake almost the last day of his life? *p.150 A moose attacks him.*

3. How is Brian's experience with the moose the opposite of what he experienced with the bear and the wolf? *Brian doesn't see the moose before it attacks him for no reason; he sees and fears the other animals but they leave him alone.*

4. How does Brian suddenly lose everything? What is his reaction? How would you feel and what would you do in his place? *pp. 156-157 A tornado destroys his shelter and fish enclosure. Brian refuses to be defeated and decides to rebuild.*

5. Why does Brian try to say some words for the pilot after the tornado? Does he find words? What words might you use? *pp. 159-160 The tornado raises the airplane's tail out of the lake, reminding Brian of the pilot inside. He concentrates on "Have rest forever."*

**Writing Activity/ Game Idea**     Write a telegram of 10 words or more. Remember: you should use only the most important words to describe your emergency. Write the telegram on a piece of paper that is two square inches in area so that you can fit it into a bottle you find on the plane.

**Prediction**     Now that the tornado has destroyed so much, what will Brian have to do?

**Chapters 17-18 pages 161-183**

**Vocabulary**

| | | |
|---|---|---|
| incessant 161 | virtually 161 | crudely 162 |
| stymied 168 | pronounced 170 | wisps 170 |
| eddy 171 | rivets 171 | experimental 174 |
| visibility 175 | substantial 178 | formers 180 |
| coupled 182 | | |

Make a three-frame cartoon about one of the following:
—something or someone that tortures you incessantly
—a time you were stymied
—a time there was nothing substantial in your refrigerator

**Discussion Questions and Activities**

1. After the tornado, what problem does Brian attack first? *p.161 He builds a fire.*

2. When is it that Brian decides to try to get into the plane? What does he hope to find? Why hasn't he tried to find it earlier? *p.163 It is after the tornado has raised the plane that Brian sees the plane's body, intact, and concludes that the survival pack must also be intact.*

3. Why does Brian build a raft? *p.166 He plans to float it out to the plane and use it as a working base while trying to get inside.*

4. Brian faces a problem when making the raft. What is it? How does he use what he learned making the walls of his shelter to solve the problem of the raft? *p.166 He realizes that by weaving logs together as he did for his wall, he can keep the pieces of the raft together.*

5. What solution does Brian come up with for keeping the raft in place by the plane? *p.168 He uses strips from his windbreaker to make a rope.*

6. What does Brian visualize his mother doing? What does this show you about the kind of person she is? *p.169 He pictures her cooking, watching TV in the kitchen, commenting on how bad the news is or how cute a baby is.*

7. How does Brian decide to get inside the plane? Why does he have to dive to the bottom of the lake first? Do you think Brian's decision to risk making the dive was a good decision? *p.174 He decides to cut his way through with his hatchet, which he drops.*

8. What does Brian see that upsets him so much? *p.180 The fish have eaten most of the flesh from the pilot's head.*

**Art/Writing Activity**

Use colored chalk on wet paper to draw something Brian sees while he is under the water. Write a short poem describing the experience. Your poem might include images (descriptions of what he sees, what he feels, what he hears...) as well as emotions.

**Literary Analysis/ Writing Activity**

Stream-of-consciousness is a method used by some authors to show you what a character is thinking. The author's sentences, like real thoughts, may be in jumbled fragments. Find an example of stream-of-consciousness in the two chapters you have read. (Sample: p.172 "...Even that—just a candy bar. It would be worth it. But how to get at the inside of the plane?") Then experiment with writing an example of your own, based on your thoughts as you sit at your desk.

**Literary Analysis Similes**

A simile uses "like" or "as" to show how two different things are alike. For example (p.162): The storm had torn the forest to pieces—up in back of the ridge it looked like a giant had become angry and used some kind of a massive meatgrinder on the trees." What two things are being compared? (the forest after the storm, and the way trees might look if they were put through a meatgrinder) How are the two things alike? (In both cases, the trees are torn into pieces.)

**Prediction**          What will Brian find in the survival pack?

**Chapter 19
and Epilogue
pages 184-195**

**Vocabulary**          epilogue          furor

How is an epilogue different from a prologue? *One comes after the book, the other before*

How is a furor different from a fury? (A furor is a frenzy or outburst, often of enthusiasm; a fury is an outburst, but of anger.)

1. What does Brian find in the survival bag? Does he find what he had hoped? *pp. 184-185 He finds many wonderful things: all he had hoped for—the fishing equipment, food, knives, matches, sleeping bag, fishing gear—and more—a knife, a compass, a first-aid kit, soap, a cap, a gun, and an emergency transmitter.*

2. How does Brian feel about the gun? Why do you think he feels that way? Are your feelings about guns similar to his, or are they different? *p.186 The gun makes him feel strange, removed from his surroundings and from all that he has learned about Nature.*

3. Why isn't Brian very excited about finding a transmitter? *He tries a switch and decides the transmitter is broken.*

4. What is on the menu of Brian's feast? What would you choose to make first, if you were in his place? *Brian makes beef and potatoes, peach whip, and orange drink.*

5. What happens to interrupt Brian's dinner? How does Brian react? *p.190 A plane flies overhead, and lands on the beach, in front of a shocked Brian.*

6. Why does this pilot find Brian when so many others had not? *p.190 The pilot had picked up the emergency transmission sent accidentally by Brian while he was trying the switches, earlier.*

7. Why is it a good thing that the pilot finds Brian when he does? *p.194 Brian would have had a lot of difficulty getting enough food once the Canadian winter set in.*

8. Name three ways the experience has changed Brian forever. Are the changes positive or negative? Can you think of any ways he may have changed that are not mentioned in the book? *pp.192-193 He will always be lean, he will always have keener observational powers than before, and he will never take food for granted again.*

9. On what topics does Brian do research after he returns home? *p.193 He wants to learn about the plants and animals he found.*

10. What sorts of dreams does Brian have after returning home? Why do you think he doesn't have nightmares? *p.194 The dreams are not frightening; he remembers the fire, the fish, the lake.*

11. Why do you think Brian doesn't tell his father the Secret. Do you think he should? Why or why not?

12. Write the imaginary transcript for one of the tapes made during an interview with Brian after the crash.

**Vocabulary:**

| | | |
|---|---|---|
| oblivious 184 | antiseptic 185 | rummaging 187 |
| drone 190 | furor 194 | |

**Discussion Questions and Activities**

**Post Reading Questions**

1. In what part of the story would you have wanted to be Brian? Why?

2. What did Brian usually think about when he was remembering his life before the crash? What do you suppose you would think about if you were in a situation like his?

3. What new problems could Brian have had, but luckily never did?

4. What particular part or parts of the story made you want to find out what was going to happen next? Why?

5. Do you think <u>Hatchet</u> is a good title for the book? Make up a new title for the story. Why did you give the story the title that you did?

6. Do you know of another story similar to this one? What is it? How is it similar? How is it different?

7. What would you change about this story if you were going to write it? Why?

8. Have you or anyone you have read or heard about ever had an experience like Brian's? What?

9. What other books, if any, have you read by this author? In what ways were they like this one?

10. This book was named as a Newbery Honor Book, a very high honor that only the best young people's books receive. Do you think the book deserved the honor? Why or why not?

**Post Reading Activities**

1. If you were to talk to the author, what questions would you ask him about the book? Make up a list of questions. Write the letter, address it, and send it.

2. If you were the artist in charge of making three illustrations for the book, what three scenes would you illustrate? Use markers or paints to make the illustrations.

3. Why do you think the author ended with the information he gave in the Epilogue? Do you think the book would be just as good if it had ended with chapter 19? Write a new ending for the story.

4. Illustrate a new book jacket for <u>Hatchet.</u> Include a cover illustration, imaginary "rave review" blurbs on the back cover, and a short biography of the author (see your librarian for reference books containing summary biographies of children's authors).

5. With a partner, make up a small booklet of math problems based on the story. For example, if Brian burned two logs every three hours, how many logs would he need to put on the fire before going on an eight-hour hunting trip?

6. Do a short research paper on one of the plants or animals Brian met, such as choke cherries or grouse.

7. Write a short, short story about how Brian's parents acted and felt during the time that Brian was lost.

8. What career might Brian decide to pursue when he is older? Make up a "help wanted" ad that Brian might answer.

9. Draw an imaginary map labeling locations mentioned in the story, such as the site of the crash, where Brian built his shelter, where he met the moose, etc.. (These maps might be collected into a bulletin board display.)

10. What sorts of dreams do you suppose Brian had during the days after the crash? Illustrate what you imagine, and label your drawing. (These might be put up on a bulletin board.)

11. The pilot who found Brian was a fur buyer mapping Cree trapping camps. Do some research to find out where these camps might be and locate on a map of Canada where you think Brian's plane crashed.

12. Choose the part of the story that you found the most tense or suspenseful. Find some music that you think expresses the feeling of the story at that point. Read that section of the story on the tape, with background music. Add the tape to a classroom listening library.

13. Suppose the furor had NOT died within a few months after Brian was found. Suppose that a MOVIE was made about Brian's experience. Create a movie poster to advertise the story. Be sure to include a picture and words that will make viewers want to see the movie. Don't forget to name the star of the movie. (These might be displayed on a bulletin board.)

14. The chapters do not have titles. Make up a title for each of the 19 chapters. Remember that a chapter title usually summarizes what happens in the chapter, or refers to an important incident or object in the chapter.

15. Make a collage about Brian's survival experience. You may use magazine cut-outs, drawings of your own, and real objects, such as twigs, feathers, berries, etc.

16. Suppose the pilot had survived. Write a short composition about what might have happened.

17. **Plot**: Choose three events in the story, and write two or three paragraphs about how changing these events would have changed what happened in the story. For example, how might the story have turned out differently if Brian had found the survival pack soon after the crash, if the transmitter really had been broken, and if the moose had broken Brian's leg?

18. Using a shoe box, clay, and various other materials of your choice such as fabric and bits of yarn, make a diorama showing a scene in the book where Brian learns something new. Include a short written explanation of what is shown.

19. Make an illustrated calendar showing important days in Brian's survival ordeal. (Bulletin board idea.)

20. Make a mobile showing some of the plants and animals Brian meets. Use a coat hanger for the base, and use thread to attach objects made from styrofoam, pieces of egg carton, and other light materials, to the base.

21. To get a better understanding of how the point of view affects a story, tell each of the following sections of the story from the given point of view.

    —Pretend you are Brian's mother. Describe what the drive to the airport is like.

    —Pretend you are Brian's father. Describe your divorce.

    —Pretend you are Brian. Describe what it is like to be so depressed that you try to commit suicide.

22. **THEME**: A central theme is an important message the author is trying to send about one of life's truths. Write a composition that mentions specific incidents from the story that support one of the following themes:

    —You should try to fit in with nature, not conquer it.

    —It never does any good to feel sorry for yourself.

—Patience and thinking are an important part of doing things right.

—To solve a problem, keep calm and think positively.

—You should try to learn from your mistakes.

—There are some secrets you should always keep.

23. Write a short essay about Brian's philosophy of life. In other words, explain why you do or do not agree with his ideas about the best attitude to take. Use specific examples to show why readers should accept your opinion.

24. Try recreating something Brian builds or makes, using the materials he had at hand, such as the fire, the spear, or even the lean-to.

25. **Setting**: Join the words or phrases on each of the lines, below, adding words of your own, to form a sentence about a setting (time and place) in <u>Hatchet</u>.

| | | |
|---|---|---|
| in the air | the plane | the pilot |
| in the lake | Brian | a stand of brush |
| in the shelter | a porcupine | the hatchet |

26. **Character**: Make a list of six adjectives that describe Brian and include something from the story to show why you chose each adjective.

27. Write a newspaper article that appears the day of the crash. Be sure to include a headline and tell **Who, What, When, Why, Where.**

28. Imagine that Brian DOES decide to tell his father the Secret. With a partner, improvise (act out) how the conversation might go.